DEDICATION

To Amanda, Fannie, Sophie, and Nella

III.25

By the practice of samyama
On the strength of an elephant
And other animals
One gains a corresponding strength.

—Yoga Sutras of Patanjali, interpreted by Mukunda

ANIMAL VEGETABLE

by Charles Levenstein

Animal Vegetable
Published through Lulu Press, Inc.

Interior Book Design and Layout by
www.integrativeink.com

Photo credit:
Mardi Tuminaro

ISBN: 978-1-4303-0156-1

ACKNOWLEDGEMENTS

Ellen Loeb
Mark Schorr
Rosy Gonzales

CONTENTS

PREFACE

Not a great oak with acorns and leaves,
Not a great dog shedding hairs left and right,
Not even a porcupine leaving spines behind:

I apologize to the walked-upon grass,
I beg forgiveness from the mowed-upon lawn,
Please forgive me oh spit-into river and spit-from bridge.

I will walk lightly to spare the ants,
I will speak softly and give others a chance,
I will suppress my cold tongue and water the plants.

Amen.

I. Vegetable

THE MARKET

Some say that summer has finished,
The sun is falling, hints of winter
Are in chill air, and the rain here
Is not soft, it insists on attention.

Then the sky clears, the mind
Forgets clues, loses all subtlety,
The sun, that lying harlot with plans,
Warms and seduces, I love you she says.

In the market her progeny, tomatoes, squash,
Peas still in their pods, lie waiting
Like Romanian orphans, Choose me!
Says the string bean, I long to adorn your stew!

I say, fill your basket! Golden corn,
Small round spuds with purple skin,
Boston leaves, mesculun, even spinach –
Fill your basket, sun is more fickle than words!

ARTICHOKES

Artichokes have a way of sneaking in,
subversive as the mysterious aubergine –

But a straightforward pizza which has resisted
Hawaiian pineapple, pine nuts, even mustard greens,

somehow opens its arms to the leafy intruder
with pickled heart, Margarita is innocent --

An honest mistake, marinated, next it will be
cauliflower and a tawdry life of vegetable excess.

GREENS

Lettuce is so frivolous –
    But perhaps I've gone too far.

Iceberg is a solid citizen.

Mesculun, despite its name, dispenses
    No hallucinations, gets me no closer
    To god or other supreme vegetarians.

Mustard greens, now they are like salt,
    Down home folks, something you can
    Sit down with and talk –

As opposed to snooty sprouts or high falutin'
    Watercress delicately presented in
    Sandwiches with circumcised crust.

I prefer spinach, baby or adult,
    Spinach gives you your money's worth,
    Can be cooked or laid out naked,
    And in either case, is beautiful
    And does the job.

My father claimed greens are for rabbits,
    But it is not true:
    They feed the people.

AGAINST ROOTS

The idea of eating roots is not appealing,
Perhaps an overly squeamish reaction
Similar to insisting on closed doors, shades
Drawn after five, ironed handkerchiefs,

And my real objection is not to carrots,
Although they need not make such a display,
Potatoes are more discreet and turnips
Can hold up their heads anywhere! No,

It's the disturbing peanut, who hangs
About in bars, mixes with other nuts
Of higher caste, the gracious walnut,
Distinguished cashew, the leechee –

Peanut, not even a root! is a social climber,
It's latest presumption to hang about with
Organic foods and, unpreserved, three days later,
A lethal poison, a terrorist, not to be trusted.

Sleeping With Mary Oliver

"All summer I made friends
  with the creatures nearby — "
Mary Oliver, "The Chance to Love Everything"
in Dream Work, 1986

On the night stand waits her dream book,
near the Tums, by the fat man's mask,
dollop of peace to ease his travels.

And in the morning there she is again,
with insect miracles of the garden,
even for the trowel-less.

II. ANIMAL

LOVE STORIES: KAFKA

Frog had been reading too much Kafka,
thought that when she kissed him
he would become something else,
if not a prince, at least not green and warty.

Turns out, she liked him covered with lichen,
hopping about, popping juicy flies in his mouth,
unemployed and sunning by the pond:
she was swamping, he craved middle class comfort.

Couldn't possibly work out, although
he did improve his English and learned to use a fork.
She, tired of leaving her eggs in a sac,
married an herpetologist and went to law school.

LOVE STORIES: WEASEL

Weasel was out that night, feeling lonely.
He saw her watching the night sky,
slinked onto the porch and ruffed
like a dog. She had her eyes on the stars,

reached to pet the soft fur brushing her leg,
never really looked into his eyes.
He was lonely (so you can't really blame him),
was willing to pass as a cocker spaniel

at least for a while. In the morning
he said that he had to get home to his wife
and kits. She cried when she realized
he was such a weasel.

TALICAT

Blind Sophie burrows under the down quilt
for her morning game, Undercover Cat.
Today, she explores the caves of Tora Bora:
She strikes swiftly and quietly, OW!
yells Ellen, breaking radio silence.
The terrocat bites, slips off the end of the bed,
escapes to Islamicat. Fat thing,
no suicide bomber.

Most Wanted: a tortoise-shell Talicat,
without Western scruples and apolitical,
bites the hand that feeds her.

BLUE BIRD BLUES

If I were a blue jay and fluffed myself up
every day before your window, would you say
I was vain? That my efforts to impress were
hopeless? Would you dismiss my ruffling
as vanity raised to an art? Can it be true
that from the start my display in this vein
was in vain, you preferred decorum
in your birds?

In defense of foolishness, I offer a pride
of lions! No one sneers at their noble mien
or, at least, cares to tell of it. If I had a ruff
like Simba, would you love me? If I had a mane,
would it still be in vain?

Ah well, vanity precedes the fall, a lovely season,
not to mention that lovely desk on which
your perfume sits. To say I'm vain suggests
that I will fail, yet I know you will love me!

LOVE IN THE FOREST: WOODPECKER

Sometime in the distant past
predators drove woodpeckers up a tree
where they lunched on beetles and birch beer.
Yet nameless fear endures and after each bite,
she swivels her head quickly about:
counts the bugs and categorizes them.
counts the branches, leaves,
assesses the breeze,
measures humidity,
eschews subjectivity,
seeks objectivity and association,
if not causal relations.

Of course she loves him, but keeps
a mate in spare; her feathers
never touch him in public. Still,
the forest whispers.

LOVE IN THE FOREST: OWL

He knows the right questions to ask,
not where, or what, or even when,
but who! And the forest sighs,
appreciating his wisdom. So for thirty
years or so, Owl repeated his query
first from the lower branches;
seniority alone would have raised him,
but the intensity of his quest,
the aura surrounding investigations
of human agency, social class,
dialectical relationships,
diabolical stewardships,
slave holders and sailing ships,
and some skill at owl-ish politics.
When he finally retired
from his lofty perch, almost
forgotten the original question:
Who, who is she?

PIGEON

Mid the doves is a runaway,
escaped the city rooftops,
tries to make a life in the bush.
He misses the ruckus of his friends,
the traffic, the lights, bagels at the deli
at any hour of the night, the theatre.
She calls him her Walter Pigeon
and for that he abandoned it all.

BLONDES: THE LIONESS

She was a contradiction:
tiny lioness with cascading blonde curls,
face that had been through the acne wars,
scarred and mottled.
Her lover was a giant Circassian,
they played throughout the house,
giggles and screams,
clomping around and sneak attacks,
unlikely friends and lovers.
Christmas was gala,
angels in the snow.

In the spring, lioness went to the mountains,
ostensibly to see her parents;
then a cruise to the Caribbean
to get a little space.
Her blonde, blue eyes appeared
in the personals seeking
an orthodox accountant
who wanted babies.
All the girlish jokes about turkey basters
for naught; last we saw her,
hair covered, dragging a three-year old
through the civic center.

BLONDES: CYNOMYS LUDOVICIANUS

Born on a Brooklyn latifundium,
studied philosophy at Harvard,
then bored with Wittgenstein,
turned to film. She was from
the Sciuridae family, Italian Jews,
and had money. A marriage made in
Gan Eden.   Their fur grew thicker
and more golden, tails luxuriant black,
they were the plumpest couple
in Cambridge. She played the cello,
he indulged in cinema verite.

She had a torrid affair with a chipmunk.

Yet through the years, our prairie dogs
stayed together, raised two pups, broke
their own and other's hearts, lived well.

In the late 1970's they moved north to farm.
A life made simple by cash.

BLONDES: EXQUISITE

Two exquisite blondes, hair blown by the wind,
sat in a convertible in the United Nations
parking lot, and worried:

We'll have to change our names, our hairdressers,
that diamond collar will have to go, I simply cannot
be called Ali – how about "Alex", I could still respond
to that. Ah, to have been born an Irish setter!

Abdul replied: *I will not dye my hair! I refuse*
to succumb to war hysteria; we survived the slurs
on our sexual orientation! If you twitch your eyes
at that greyhound one more time, you will sing
the castrato's part in a Christian choir!

We petition the Kennel Club
to re-name the "Afghan".
We are monarchist hounds
and bark by divine right.
How about Northern Alliance Dog?
How about Coalition Canine?

COFFEE BREAK

Fidget is a morning bird,
by break time needs his coffee
and a bun, all dietary resolve
dissipated, hops from
stool to counter, hopes
for short order service.

Fuss too tired to jump,
whines about the office,
indicts the maid, heat, careless
fellow workers, last night's dinner,
her husband's business trips,
the cost of hormone replacement.

Season after season, these budgies
meet at 10:30AM, no one seems
to know why or when it started,
an old accountant claims
chubby fellow and nasty biddy once
were young and ferocious lovers.

I serve their coffee, danish for him,
biscotti for her; she dunks,
he nibbles, I see their ease,
no new foibles to discover, she reaches
to brush a crumb from his cheek,
he smiles and chirps his thanks.

CROCODILE TEARS

I've always wondered
if a denizen differs from
a resident in any significant
way; and how inhabitant
spawned co-habitant or
vice versa. These my thoughts
as I circumnavigate the swamp
-- some say wetlands but
I say bullrush when I see one --
and some mistake
the silent movement of my lips
as I mouth these words
for hostility. How unfortunate!

The ways of the crocodile poet
are subject to misinterpretation
based on misinformation, prejudice
and stereotype. My skin is thick
but I feel, my tears are real!
If you think my eyes bulge,
let me show you haiku born
of such opthamological capability:
I attend, I see, I can lie
for hours and contemplate a lizard.
My teeth are large, tongue formidable,
but do you disparage the elephant,
whose molars are hidden
by that ridiculous trunk?

Ah what's the use! Humanity
is characterized by its abuse
of the likes of me! My skin holds
your money, your pants would
fall without my help, your feet
are adorned with the texture of my
life, but you scorn my aspirations.
Don't wonder, then, when you sit

in thin-skinned boats
in khaki shorts
in search of nature,
that your stature only brings to mind
breakfast, lunch and dinner.

THE FINCH FABLE

Everyone thought the finches
would grow old together;
they shared a bamboo cage
by the window, watched
as the leaves changed on the trees,
caught the scent of spring perfumes,
delighted in summer fire flies,
even the sweet sadness of autumn
seemed to bring them closer.
In the mornings they twittered
to each other and to the world.
A simple but rewarding life

until one day the cage door was open.
Was it he or she who saw it?
No matter, one cowered and
one ventured out. In a flash
lurking tabby had mouthed its catch
and disappeared. The lazy but omniscient
writer reached beneath the couch,
dragged out the cat and freed
Sir (or Madame) Finch from his jaws.

Back in the cage, the finches eyed one another.
Are you all right?
Are you safe?
How could you leave me like that?

A wizened bird perched quietly.
Home, safe at home,
safe in the scolding,
a memory of free flight,
a memory of sharp teeth.
(I never meant to leave at all.)

This story has been passed on,
generation after generation
has heard of the cat and the writer,
a sober warning to fear strangers
and love god.

MORE LOVE STORIES: FERRET

The ferret sat at the bar sipping Jack.
Once he lost his family in a forest fire,
his tears were such that
you could almost forget
he was a ferret.
In pity, the English teacher took him home,
ostensibly for tutoring, but
both knew what was what.

Ferrets slip up and down your sleeves,
will even settle in your crotch
if you don't watch out.
She was shocked when
she heard the rodent tell a friend
Some women are into ferrets.
He saw her face and was ashamed.

MORE LOVE STORIES: SELFISH BEAR

The brown bear meditates all winter,
emerges in the spring with cavernous appetite
and clear mind. She sees him, likes
his black eyes and gaunt face,
ferocious concentration, rapid pace;
this might be a one spring fling,
see how the summer goes;
the woods are thick with honey,
fish flood the river,
bushes sprout every kind of berry.
The fields blossom with wildflowers
in celebration of their frolics.
By the fall he's fattened and slow,
she starts to go down town
while he begins his dream of silence.
I wanted to do the tango,
He can't even fox trot,
He was a selfish bear,
And that was that.

THE FICKLE PLOVER

A snail and a plover
eyed one another, thought --
I wonder what that would be like.

Seabirds are nervous, skip about
the waves for food and fun.
Always a bigger bird
ready to steal your mussel.
Sometimes the tide brings in a morsel,
then it's swept away. Best
to check over one's shoulder.

Snail was ready to emigrate
for her plover. He was kind,
attentive, treated her like
garlicked and buttered escargot;
she thrived in the glow but
traveled at her own pace --
Finally ready, with the plover
sought legal advice.

Lawyer took Snail aside,
warned her about plover promiscuity;
Don't cast ornithological aspersions!
At 45 this bird may be my last chance!

In his office high over the harbor,
pen poised above a yellow pad,
said the lawyer: *In that case,*
when will be your wedding date?

Flying high above the harbor,
searching ground for decent cover,
fled the nervous plover lover.
Lawyer had left the window open --
Snail wept in disbelief,
but we've all known other shellfish

who have misunderstood
seabird's intentions.

Sparrow Song

The days are shorter,
still I twitter in the bush
and hope she will notice.
Winters are milder
than Decembers of my youth,
yet assuage not loneliness.

If I were like the rest of the flock
and slept with tweedle-dee or bum-de-bum,
scattered my seed to kingdom come,
perhaps the winter would seem less stark,
I would hang out in the park,
cock of the walk in a sparrow world.

The days are shorter,
still I twitter in the bush
and hope she will notice.
Winters are milder
than Decembers of my youth,
yet assuage not loneliness.

Instead, I watch her with her lovers,
chirping sweet banalities,
gaily laughing over an insect tidbit.
They frolic in the bush
snd she bestows her favors
on every shallow tweeter
who asks the time of day:
more than a tiny sparrow heart can bear!

The days are shorter,
still I twitter in the bush
and hope she will notice.
Winters are milder
than Decembers of my youth,
yet assuage not loneliness.

August is Ours!

Two white butterflies courting high above me
Spiraled down to the dense green bushes beside the road,
Were greeted by a horde of their friends:

"Hooray!
We have ended our slippery sliding crawling days!
We are not birds but we are high flyers and
a great crowd of white wood nymphs.

Say what you will,
August is ours!"

CREATURELY THINGS

The nose runs.
The tongue is swollen.
The right eye is red and leaks tears.
This frog was once my person.
Punishment for Gan Eden.

THE CHICKENHAWK'S CASE

The chickenhawk presents his case
To the feathered court of his fair race.
He pleads all day and half the night
To right wrongs done him out of spite.

"I loved her, friends, she was my treasure;
I only sought to give her pleasure.
I warmed her with her favorite dishes
And catered to her slightest wishes.

"And then one day, there came upon me
A grand compulsion that alarmed me!
My mind fixed an evil strategem
(But had I chops I'd have licked 'em).

"I will spare you the squawks and hollers:
I had my bird with beans and collards,
Dry red wine with all went well,
My lovely dove was really swell.

"Now: If I were feline, a hunting cat,
Wouldn't you meow and give a pat?
Would you cast me from the house,
If I stalked a rat or a pretty brown mouse?

"So please, dear friends, do not squawk
At the noble bird, the chickenhawk.
If you must, warn the neighbor's dove,
Don't mistake hunger for undying love!

"The moral of the story, friends of chickens:
If you want to avoid being some bird's pickin's,
Stick with the rooster, who may be a pain,
But you won't become his coq au vin."

The feathered jury conversed all night,
But found no answer to this chirpish plight.

Hawks eat doves when they get a chance,
It's only humans who prefer to dance.

P.S.

LETTER TO ABE

*"I think that when we spent a lot of time together,
I did not know much about you ...."*

We met in the morning,
when sex, power and friendship are served
like brunch, two eggs over easy,
bacon on the side.

By noon you were a favorite for the women:
boy genius, Yiddish poet, Chomsky in your pocket
and great curly hair. I was playing Swami Bar Mitzvah,
revolutionary sandwich; in truth,
grieving for my son. When the war was ended,
we lost the peace.

Between denial breaks and self-delusion, investigated
free love, expensive love, ridiculously extortionate love;
you were miserable, soulful.
I was just a jerk.

I can't remember dinner.
I was probably drunk.
You went home
with all the other abandoned folks.
I reformed, became an orange mandarin,
the marmalade of my late mother's eye.

So here we are with virtual cigars and brandy.
Talking sex is something young bears do;
power is an electric company problem.
Friendship and time are all what's left.